IPHONE 15

PRO MAX CAMERA

USER GUIDE

The Complete iPhone 15 Pro Max Camera Manual For Beginners Seniors And Professional Content Creators With Pictures. With Photo Editing Tips And Tricks

By

Williams M. Brown

Table Of Contents

INTRODUCTION

At first appearance, the iPhone 15 Pro Max (beginning at $1,199) may seem to be a minor upgrade to Apple's flagship smartphone, but it surprises with its powerful performance. The iPhone 15 Pro Max has a lot going for it, including a more streamlined design, faster processing speed, a useful Action button, and strong software. While the move from Apple's proprietary Lightning connector to the more widely used USB-C may seem long overdue, it actually enhances the iPhone's functionality in several unexpected ways. When you compare the smaller iPhone 15 Pro with the larger

15 Pro Max—which has better battery life, a greater camera zoom range, and more basic storage—it becomes evident that the 15 Pro Max is the greatest iPhone for power users and serious producers.

PROS

✓ Fast, smooth performance
✓ Excellent cameras
✓ Long battery life
✓ Useful Action button
✓ USB-C connectivity opens up new features
✓ Lighter than previous Pro Max

CONS

✗ Expensive
✗ Big

APPLE IPHONE 15 PRO MAX SPECS

Operating System	iOS 17
CPU	Apple A17 Pro
Dimensions	6.29 by 3.02 by 0.32 inches
Screen Size	6.7 inches
Screen Resolution	2796 by 1280 pixels
Camera Resolution (Rear; Front-Facing)	48MP/12MP/12MP;12MP
Battery Life (As Tested)	20 hours 15 minutes

A New Port Of Entry

You wouldn't know it from looking at the iPhone 15 Pro Max, but it's the most significant design update to the phone since the 2020 iPhone 12 series. From a distance of a few feet, the 15 Pro Max resembles the 14 Pro Max, 13 Pro Max, and 12 Pro Max quite a bit. But there are a lot of changes that become apparent when you look closely.

The first change is the frame's new form and substance. Titanium and somewhat softened edges replace the sharp angles and stainless steel of the 14 Pro Max. Titanium, according to Apple, is both stronger and lighter. The former is true without a doubt, but we have not conducted tests on it. Noticeably lighter than the 14 Pro Max at 7.81 ounces is the 15 Pro Max. This may not seem like much, but it makes a huge impact in the actual world. Also, at 6.29 by 3.02 by 0.32 inches (HWD), the 15 Pro Max is somewhat smaller than its predecessor, which was 6.33 by 3.05 by 0.31 inches. The phone is much more comfortable to carry and use now that its hardware is smaller and lighter and has rounded edges.

The iPhone 15 Pro, which retails for $999 and starts at 5.77 by 2.78 by 0.32 inches, is 6.6 ounces lighter and smaller. Starting at $899, the 15 iPhone Plus is 7.09 ounces heavier and 0.01 inch bigger and taller than the 15 Pro Max. In comparison to Apple's newest, the top-selling Android gadget from Samsung, the Galaxy S23 Ultra, weighs 8.25 ounces and measures 6.43 by 3.07 by 0.35 inches (with prices beginning at $1,199), making it larger and heavier. This year's iPhone Pro versions are available in four different titanium colors: black, blue, natural, and white.

When it comes to smartphone manufacturers, the iPhone 15 Pro Max has the best fit and quality.

While fingerprints may sometimes alter the titanium's color, the material's fine grain and matte finish make it a notable improvement over prior versions' highly polished stainless steel. Even now, Apple's front glass has Ceramic Shield, while the back features textured matte glass. It states that they are more durable than the majority of smartphone glass options. Smartphones that compete with the iPhone use Corning Gorilla Glass Victus or Victus+. These include the Galaxy S and Pixel series. Like any high-end flagship, the iPhone 15 Pro Max has an IP68 certification that protects it from dust and water. So, your phone will be OK after a short dip in the pool or stream, and you can even wash it off if it becomes filthy. (A protective cover is still a must-have for a phone of this price, however.)

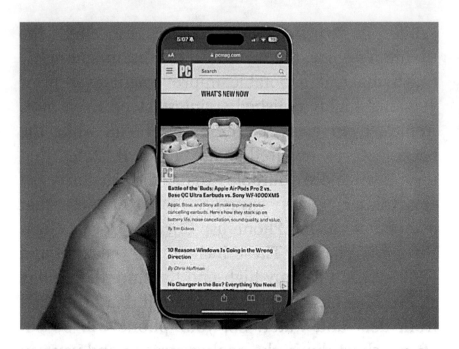

On the outside of the phone, you can see two of the most notable hardware upgrades. To start, the power/screen lock button is located on the right side of the phone, as it usually is. Both the travel and feedback of this button are flawless. The individual volume controls on the left side function in the same way. What sets it apart? Both the Lightning port on the bottom and the ringer switch on the left side are no longer there.

An Action button, formerly used as a ringer switch, has been added to this year's Pro iPhones by Apple. Toggle between quiet and ring modes with a long press of the Action button, which still controls the ringer by default. However, following in the footsteps of its Android rivals, Apple allows iPhone Pro users to personalize the behavior of this button. Launch the camera, activate the flashlight, record a voice note, switch to Focus Mode, activate the magnifier, toggle an accessibility feature, or enable your own shortcut—among many other functions— that you may program it to do. There are a lot of potential novel applications for this final choice. By using Apple's Shortcuts feature, you can do tasks like as opening your garage door or controlling smart home devices like lighting by just pressing the Action button. Launching Shazam to discover the title of nearby playing music was a breeze once I had it set up. The possibilities are endless, so enjoy yourself. The button's rather odd placement on the left edge makes it the only negative.

Instead of the older Lightning connector, the bottom edge of every iPhone 15 device now has a USB-C connection. Because of an EU regulation requiring the use of a single charging cable for all smartphones and certain other gadgets, Apple was compelled to make this adjustment. The goal is to lessen the burden on customers while simultaneously decreasing electronic waste. Regardless, the iPhone 15 now comes with a USB-C connector, which is capable of a wide range of functions.

If you own AirPods Pro or an Apple Watch Series 9, for instance, you may charge them from your iPhone using this feature. As an added bonus, the 15 Pro Max and 15 Pro include a connector that allows you to record 4K60 ProRes footage straight from your iPhone to an external SSD. For certain kinds of artists, that's a huge boon. Input devices like cameras and microphones may be attached to the iPhone for recording audio or video, and direct connections to 4K60 HDR screens can be made to mirror the iPhone's screen for gaming or watching movies.

While there is no shortage of Lightning-based accessories for earlier iPhone models, the selection of USB-C accessories that are compatible with the iPhone 15 series is far more extensive. Both of the 15 Pro variants are compatible with the USB-C 3 Gen 2 standard, which allows for data transfer rates of up to 10Gbps. In comparison, the non-Pro iPhone 15 models only support USB-C 2.0, which has a maximum limit of 480Mbps. On the other hand, USB-C has been around for a long time for Android phones.

Even while the iPhone 15 Pro Max is still clearly an iPhone and the improvements don't seem substantial at first glance, iPhone users will feel the long-term benefits of Apple's decision to change materials, buttons, and ports.

Numerous Pixels

This year, Apple hasn't made any major changes to the screens of the Pro range. The two Pro versions retain the majority of features from the previous generation, but the plain iPhone 15 and 15 Plus do away with the notch and get access to the Dynamic Island. The only noticeable improvement is that Apple has trimmed the bezels a millimeter or two on either side. This contributes to the somewhat lower size of the 15 Pro models compared to their 14 Pro predecessors and also implies that there is less black border around the screen.

The diagonal of the phone's 6.7-inch Super Retina XDR screen has 2,796 by 1,290 pixels, or 460 pixels per inch. A 6.1-inch screen with 2,556 by 1,179 pixels yields the same pixel density of 460ppi as the larger 15 Pro. In layman's terms, the screen features an adjustable refresh rate that ranges from 1Hz all the way up to 120Hz, thanks to Apple's ProMotion technology. The phone's scrolling experience is now more fluid as a result. On top of that, it has extensive color support over the whole P3 gamut and supports automated True Tone white balancing to match the surrounding light. Brightness levels of

1,000 nits (normal), 1,600 nits (HDR peak), and 2,000 nits (outdoor peak) are maintained, and the contrast ratio stays at 2,000,000:1. For those sunny outdoor days, this phone is perfect for enjoying movies on the go. Even in very bright light, I could make out every detail on the screen.

The Samsung Galaxy S23 Ultra, in contrast, has a 6.8-inch Dynamic AMOLED 2x Infinity-O screen, 120Hz, 3,088 by 1,440 pixels, and 501 pixels per inch. A 6.7-inch OLED display with 3,210 by 1,440 pixels and a somewhat higher pixel density of 512ppi is available on the $999 Google Pixel 7 Pro. Although it lacks the Pro Max's fast refresh rate and always-on display, the iPhone 15 Plus shares the Pro Max's screen size and resolution.

By the way, Apple hasn't really upgraded the Pro models' Dynamic Island or always-on display. While more and more apps—like United and Uber—are supporting Dynamic Island activities, more and more apps—like Lyft and YouTube Music—are supporting home screen widgets.

The module that enables Face ID and the user-facing camera are both located on the Dynamic Island. The iPhone's face unlock feature is among the greatest in its field, and it's also the only biometric security option available. It unlocks the phone reliably and swiftly regardless of the illumination. In fact, it can take into consideration alterations to your face including beards, spectacles, caps, and face masks. Both the S23 Ultra and the Pixel 7 Pro, like the majority of Android phones, use fingerprint readers for biometrics.

Power To Spare

New iPhones and processors are introduced annually by Apple. This year, it follows a different naming scheme from previous year's A16 Bionic and is referred to as the A17 Pro. With its 6-core design consisting of two performance cores and four efficiency cores, this new chip is 10% quicker than the A16. It is based on a 3nm technology. Although Apple does not provide the exact clock speeds, testing programs indicate that the top core operates at 3.77GHz. In addition to a 16-core Neural Engine that is twice as quick at machine learning tasks as the A16, the A17 Pro has a fresh new six-core GPU that is 20% quicker. With features like hardware-accelerated ray tracing, Apple claims the A17 Pro will significantly boost mobile gaming performance. The ProMotion display, AV1 decoder, and high-speed USB are all aspects of the phone that are made possible by the processor.

You may choose between 256GB, 512GB, or 1TB of storage on the iPhone 15 Pro Max. Although Apple removed the 128GB model from the Max range, which resulted in a $100 increase to the Pro Max line's basic price, the option to have that much storage is still available for the smaller 15 Pro. Our test model has 8 GB of RAM, according to benchmark programs; nevertheless, Apple does not provide this information. The basic amount of RAM and these storage choices are comparable to competitive smartphones. Eight gigabytes of random access memory (RAM) should be more than enough for an iOS device, even if some high-end

Android phones have twelve or sixteen gigabytes of RAM. And our testing confirms it.

While it's not exactly an apples-to-apples comparison, we can still get a good idea of how the iPhone 15 Pro Max stacks up against its competitors by comparing it to Android benchmarks.

On the single-core test, the iPhone 15 Pro Max scored 2,928 and on the multi-core test, it scored 7,268 according to Geekbench 6, which measures CPU power. That significantly outperforms the Galaxy S23 Ultra's 1,545 and 5,078 points in Geekbench 5.5 as well as the iPhone 14 Pro Max's 1,874 and 5,445 points. In contrast, the Pixel 7 Pro managed dismal scores of 1,050 and 3,190. Snapdragon 8 Gen 2 powers the Galaxy, while Tensor G2 powers the Pixel.

Then, we performed many iterations of the graphics-focused GFXBench test, which includes T-Rex, Manhattan, and Aztec Ruins. In all three tests, Apple's gadget averaged 60 frames per second, although the Galaxy S23 Ultra and the iPhone 14 Pro Max both achieved speeds of 62 and 54 frames per second, respectively. Notably, Apple showed an improvement of almost 11% over the previous year.

In 3DMark, we saw that the phone achieved an average frame rate of 22 frames per second and a score of 3,634. The phone seems to outperform 85 percent of other devices tested with 3DMark, including the 3,377 points scored by the iPhone 14 Pro Max.

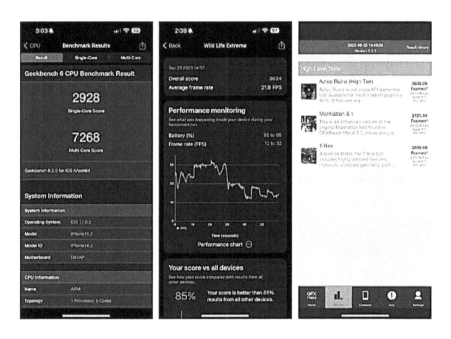

Resident Evil Village, an upcoming iOS game that utilizes the A17 Pro, was given early access by Apple. With constant frame rates and jitter-free action, the game looks great on the screen of the iPhone 15 Pro Max. Even though the phone became rather hot by the end of the game, the lighting is really stunning.

The 15 Pro Max never froze when using professional software like GarageBand, Lightroom, and iMovie, in addition to the usual suspects like Safari, Mail, Messages, and the camera.

As the iPhone 15 Pro Max (and the same CPU as the iPhone 15 Pro), power is not an issue. The A16 Bionic chip, which is a year old, causes the 15 Plus and 15 to be somewhat slower.

An Electrical Monster

When it comes to battery life, the Pro Max is head and shoulders above the competition. Although Apple does not provide the exact dimensions of the iPhone's battery, we may assume that the lithium-ion power cell has a capacity of around 4,400mAh, which is lower than the 5,000mAh seen in many high-end Android phones. Simply said, Apple can outperform its rivals while doing more with fewer resources.

By maximising the screen brightness and continuously streaming a YouTube movie over Wi-Fi, we ensure that every phone undergoes the same battery depletion test. We measured 20 hours and fifteen minutes of streaming video, however Apple says the 15 Pro Max can go 25 hours in this situation. Compared to last year's iPhone 14 Pro Max, which had a battery life of 19 hours, that's a significant 1.25-hour boost. It outperforms the Pixel 7 Pro's 10 hours and 30 minutes as well as the Galaxy S23 Ultra's 13 hours and 11 minutes.

The phone's real-world performance was impressive, lasting at least 1.5 days between charges. The Pro Max is the best iPhone to buy if you're concerned about the battery life of your device.

The iPhone is certified to work with 20W wired charging. Although a charging brick is no longer included in the phone's packaging, a premium braided USB-C-to-USB-C cable is. While we were able to measure a maximum charging rate of 27W for the iPhone 15 Pro Max using a high-speed brick, that is the highest pace we would recommend. Other Android phones charge more quickly; for example, the OnePlus 11 5G requires 80W whereas the S23 Ultra only needs 45W.

Our testing showed that the battery life of the 15 Pro Max was 33 minutes to get from 0% to 50%, which is somewhat longer than the 30 minutes that Apple promises. It took around 85 minutes to get the battery to 100%, which is somewhat less time than last year's model (which took 90 minutes). The OnePlus 11 5G could be completely recharged in under 27 minutes, compared to the S23's 71-minute total charging time.

With Apple's MagSafe wireless charging technology, which use magnets to assist in positioning the iPhone correctly on MagSafe charging accessories, the iPhone may be charged wirelessly. The iPhone can be fully charged in around 120 minutes using MagSafe's 15W wireless charging technology. Even regular Qi wireless chargers may be used, however their charging speed is limited to only 7.5W. During full power-ups, the phone did grow warm.

Is your Apple Watch or AirPods in need of a revitalization? Reverse charging at 4.5W is possible with the iPhone 15 Pro Max and USB-C. All versions of the iPhone 15 include that new feature.

Making (Air) Waves

The iPhone 15 Pro has an upgraded Qualcomm Snapdragon X70 modem, up from the X65 in the iPhone 14, albeit Apple has not revealed the exact model. It keeps the important C-band spectrum in the US and supports sub-6GHz and mmWave 5G. After putting the 15 Pro Max through its paces on Verizon's network in and around NYC, we were rather pleased.

In a Verizon 5G Ultra Wideband-covered region, download speeds hit 301Mbps, which is far better than the 90Mbps recorded by the iPhone 14 Pro Max in the same testing, and almost on pace with the 295Mbps recorded by an S23 Ultra. The most noteworthy development is the significant increase in upload rates, which have soared to 122Mbps, from 8.3Mbps on the iPhone 14 Pro Max. When comparing the two devices in low-signal areas, the iPhone 15 Pro Max came out on top with speeds of 21 Mbps down and 14 Mbps up, while the S23 Ultra only managed 17 Mbps down and 9.3 Mbps up.

This year, Wi-Fi receives a significant update, moving from the somewhat out-of-date Wi-Fi 6 standard to the more modern Wi-Fi 6E, the standard that the majority of flagship smartphones are embracing. We saw a peak download speed of 640Mbps when testing the phone about one foot away from a Verizon Fios router with 940Mbps service. This is comparable to the 609Mbps recorded by the S23 Ultra, but far faster than the 475Mbps recorded by the Pixel 7 Pro and the 435Mbps recorded by the iPhone 14 Pro Max. The difference between the 14 Pro Max's 209 Mbps and 239 Mbps upload speeds is hardly noticeable. When tested near the edge of the Wi-Fi network, the phone performed well, reaching 8.1 Mbps, which is lower than the S23's 6.35 Mbps.

The 15 Pro Max maintains last year's Bluetooth 5.3 connectivity. With this most recent specification, the iPhone continues to offer spatial audio in addition to AAC, Apple Lossless, and FLAC. According to our testing, genuine wireless earbuds produced excellent sound quality and maintained a stable connection even when used outside of the usual Bluetooth range.

Thread networking technology is now available on Apple's iPhone 15 Pro models. This eliminates the need for a separate hub and allows the phone to communicate directly with smart home devices that use the Thread protocol. However, Apple claims that the function will be activated in a future software update and is not now operational.

No, the SIM card tray is not making a triumphant return to Apple products. There is a limit of eight eSIM profiles that may be kept on an iPhone 15s heading for the US. Each eSIM profile can handle up to two active numbers. It took me less than a minute to transfer all of my Verizon account data from my old 14 Pro Max to my new 15 Pro Max. Your mileage may vary, according to online horror stories.

With my Verizon account, all of my phone interactions, including HD voice calls, sounded crystal clear. No problems with the network were seen throughout my testing, and the earpiece located above the screen offers sufficient loudness for conversations in any environment, whether it a crowded city street or a quiet house. By removing ambient noise, the new Voice Isolation function greatly improves your audibility while making phone calls.

With the earpiece acting as one and the bottom-firing speaker as the other, the phone has built-in stereo speakers. With well-balanced highs and lows, the majority of audiovisual information sounds fantastic when played over speakers. The Knife's "Silent Shout," the bass test track, has present low-end wallop and clear, detailed highs. When turned up to its maximum, distortion might be audible. A Bluetooth speaker is the way to go if you want your music on high volume.

Last year, the iPhone 14 series received two new features from Apple: Crash Detection and Emergency SOS. Emergency Roadside Assistance is a somewhat reduced form of the service that is being offered this year. Similar to how the iPhone can contact a satellite-based service in cellular-unreachable regions, this one can link you up with AAA to get assistance with things like vehicle battery charging or flat tire replacement, rather than a full-scale rescue. Tows and other vehicle services may cost money for those who aren't AAA members, but it's free for members. Although we did not put it through its paces, this function is free for the first two years on all iPhone 15s in the US.

Finally, we have Apple's Ultra Wideband processor, which is the second generation. For the most part, this supplementary radio serves to expand capabilities within Apple's own ecosystem. As an example, it enhances the AirPods Pro 2nd Gen with USB-C with new Find My capabilities, making it possible to locate them with pinpoint precision in the event that you lose them. Locating other iPhone 15s is also a similar process. With the most recent iPhones, the Find My app provides more exact directions and distance, allowing users to more precisely find one other while they're out and about. When tested with two iPhone 15s, this function delivered very accurate distance and direction information, bordering on terrifying.

Cameras

Apple is trying something new this year with the iPhone 15, and all of the models share the same 48MP primary camera sensor. In the past, smartphone manufacturers would often trash a 48MP sensor four times to get 12MP photos with more light. Apple asserts that this 24MP picture, which is the result of merging a binned 12MP snap with a full-size 48MP frame, offers better low-light performance and greater clarity. If you'd like, you can shoot in high quality using the HEIF and ProRAW formats on your iPhone 15.

Apple is letting users fine-tune its primary camera even more on the iPhone 15 Pro and Pro Max. Because of the massive 48MP sensor, the Pro allows artists to swiftly switch between three conventional prime lenses: 24mm (1x), 28mm (1.2x), and 35mm (1.5x). This feature must be enabled in the settings.

Apple claims that the primary camera, which uses the core 12MP of the sensor, can take photographs with a 2x "optical" zoom. It claims that this technique yields twice-zoomed images with the same level of clarity as those captured with a roughly 2x glass lens.

A 12MP ultra-wide camera with an aperture of f/2.2 is standard on all of this year's Pro iPhone models. The camera can take 0.5x superwide photos (or point-fivers as the teenagers would say) and also function as a macro lens, allowing for very close-up photographs (~2cm) of objects like flowers.

A 5x optical telephoto lens, equal to 120mm at f/2.8, is housed in the iPhone 15 Pro Max's third camera. An innovative 3D sensor-shift optical image stabilization module and a tetraprism work together to do this, with the former allowing for more light bending and extension and the latter maintaining stability at the longer focal length. A 3x optical telephoto lens, measuring in at 77mm, is available on the more compact iPhone 15 Pro.

The 12 megapixel TrueDepth front-facing camera on all iPhone 15s is identical to the primary camera.

Yeah, that's quite a few cameras. What do you think of the images? To put it simply, first-rate.

While shooting outside in natural light, the iPhone 15 Pro Max captures images that are crisp, clear, and filled with warmth. All of the images have correct color, good white balance, and fine focus. The shading and tonal highlighting are both visually appealing. The colors are well-matched whether you use the primary, telephoto, or ultra-wide lenses.

When you go inside, the situation changes somewhat. Pictures taken inside reveal a lot more background noise, especially in situations with very warm lighting.

With a few touches on the screen, you can toggle between the three lenses and the primary lens's three focal lengths; however, you can also squeeze to zoom if you like. You can zoom in and out of all three cameras without any noticeable lag on the iPhone 15 Pro.

Above, you can see a close-up of several multicolored Rice Krispies treats—proof that the ultra-wide camera excels at macro pictures.

Pictures like these of river pebbles come out very crisp from the 5x optical zoom lens. Compared to the iPhone 14 Pro Max's 3x photographs, the 5x shots are much clearer. However, the Pixel 7 Pro and Galaxy S23 Ultra both produce even finer images than the iPhone in this regard.

Even at night, the images turn out beautifully. The sky isn't overblown in this photograph of a Thai restaurant, which exhibits a lot of detail.

Selfies taken in portrait mode are noticeably different from those taken in landscape mode. The former offers a little broader field of vision with deep backgrounds, while the later gives you a pleasant amount of bokeh. In the second scenario, certain lighting effects are used to make your face seem brighter.

By the way, bokeh is something you can take use of in post-processing portraits of people, dogs, or cats with any model of iPhone 15 as it automatically records depth data. (Just like we did with the picture of the cat up there.) It's a delightful feature that provides additional flexibility in case you overlook the option to activate portrait mode.

The video capabilities of the iPhone 15 Pro Max are quite exceptional. The camera can record at a maximum of 4K60 in ProRes, and it has features like the Academy Color Encoding System, Log encoding for individualized color correction in post-processing, and 1x to 3x cinematic zoom. Not only does it include an Action mode for stabilization, but it also has a variety of slow-motion and hyperlapse recording options, and it can record straight to external hard drives via USB-C.

Even though both Samsung and Google have improved their phones recently, the iPhone still has no equal when it comes to video. You can't go wrong with the iPhone 15 Pro Max as your go-to smartphone for recording videos whether you're into vlogging or just love watching videos.

IOS Turns 17

With the release of iOS 17, Apple's newest operating system, all four of the iPhone 15 models come standard. Read our comprehensive review to learn about all the new features. Most of iOS 17's features are available on iPhones that are two generations old or later, including the XR, XS, and SE models.

Standby Mode is one of our favorites since it essentially makes your iPhone a smart display while it's charging and turned horizontally. The weather, your calendar, the time, and more can all be customized on your iPhone. The software on the iPhone 15 Pro models is identical to that on the regular iPhone 15, with the exception of some additional photography capabilities, settings for the always-on display and Action button, and a few other features.

The fact that the iPhone 15 Pro Max will continue to get security and feature upgrades for a long time is the most crucial piece of information to have. Two to four years of software upgrades and maybe one more year of security updates are provided to most Android devices. Software and security updates for the majority of iPhones are released every five years.

CHAPTER ONE

HOW TO TURN OFF AND TURN ON IPHONE

1. You'll need to press and hold the Side Button in addition to any Volume Button available.

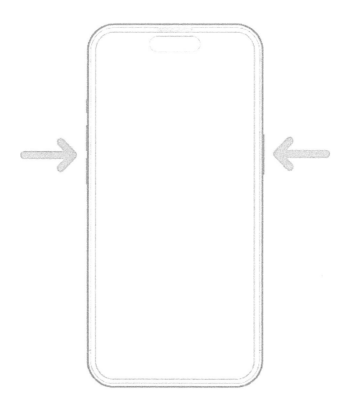

2. Maintain button presses until a slider labeled "Slide to Power Off" appears.

3. Just release the buttons and move the slider left to right.

To power down your brand new iPhone 15 Pro max, just follow these steps. Fixing system faults and glitches is as easy as following this procedure. Additionally, the Settings app on your iPhone allows you to turn it off. You may easily turn off the device by dragging the slider in the Settings > General > Shut Down menu. The outcome is independent on the method you select.

HOW TO TURN OFF SIRI ON YOUR IPHONE

Siri may be easily disabled on iOS 11 or later. Give it a try:

- Launch the Settings app on your iOS device.

- Find Section 4 and click on Siri & Search.

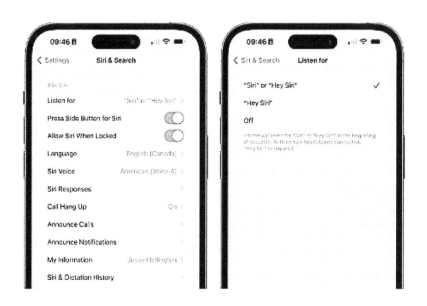

- Pick Listen for at the top of the screen if you're using iOS 17 or later. On the following screen, pick the Off option.

To disable the ability to hear Siri's voice on iOS 16 and before, turn off the corresponding setting.

- Disable the Siri side button.

- You'll get a warning that your HomePods can't identify your voice or answer to personal requests anymore if you have personal requests enabled in your house. You may confirm this by selecting Stop Using Siri.

- In the last pop-up that opens, choose Turn Off Siri.

If you do this, Siri will no longer be able to react to voice commands. But it doesn't turn off the Dictation function, as this last pop-up shows. If you would want all information pertaining to Siri erased from Apple's servers, you may do so individually by disabling it in the Settings app under General > Keyboard > Enable Dictation.

HOW TO SET UP FACE ID ON IPHONE

Simply look at your iPhone to securely unlock it, approve purchases and payments, and sign in to a plethora of third-party apps—all with Face ID (supported models).

A passcode is also required to utilize Face ID on an iPhone.

INSTALL FACE ID OR CREATE AN ALTERNATE APPEARANCE.

- Navigate to Settings > Face ID & Passcode > Set up Face ID, and then follow the onscreen instructions, in case you neglected to do so during the initial setup of your iPhone.
- Follow the on-screen steps to set up an alternate look for Face ID to recognize. You may do this by going to Settings > Face ID & Passcode > Set Up an Alternate look.

Move your head slowly to complete the circle.

Accessibility Options

Start Over

During Face ID setup, you'll have the option to tap on Accessibility Options in case you have any physical constraints. This way, you may set up face recognition without using your whole head movement. Face ID is still a safe method, but it does need you to gaze at your iPhone more consistently.

If you are visually impaired or blind, you may also utilize the accessibility function that comes with Face ID. To disable Face ID's need that you keep your eyes open while using the iPhone, head to the iPhone's Settings > Accessibility and then tap the "Require Attention for Face ID" button. When you enable VoiceOver during iPhone setup, this function is disabled by default.

USE FACE ID WHILE WEARING A FACE MASK

Wearing a face mask (or any other covering that conceals your mouth and nose) will not prevent you from using Face ID to unlock your iPhone 12, 13, 14, or 15 model.

Turning on Face ID while wearing a mask allows the feature to study the specific features around your eyes; it is compatible with all of the Face ID settings you enable in Settings > Face ID & Passcode.

Note: When you simply want to use Face ID for full-face recognition, it works the best.

Perform one of these actions after going to Settings > Face ID & Passcode:

- Make sure Face ID can still function while you're wearing a mask: Press the button that says "Face ID with a Mask" and then follow the on-screen prompts.

Note: To enhance the accuracy of Face ID, use clear glasses instead of sunglasses while using a mask. This will help if you normally wear spectacles.

- *Enhance Your Look With A Pair Of See-Through Eyeglasses (Not Sunglasses):* Select "Add Glasses," and then proceed as directed.
- *Wearing A Face Mask Will Prevent Face ID From Functioning:* Use a mask to disable Face ID.

As an alternative, you may unlock your iPhone even while wearing a face mask by using your Apple Watch in conjunction with any iPhone model that supports Face ID.

TEMPORARILY DISABLE FACE ID
If you don't want Face ID to unlock your iPhone, you may disable it temporarily.

- For two seconds, press and hold the side button in addition to both volume buttons.
- To lock your iPhone as soon as the sliders display, press and hold the side button.

If you don't touch the screen for about a minute, your iPhone will lock automatically.

Once you unlock your iPhone using the passcode, Face ID will be activated again.

DEACTIVATE FACE ID.
Select Face ID & Passcode from the Settings menu.

Choose an option from these:

- Disable Face ID for individual objects only: You may disable some of the settings.
- For use with face masks, disable Face ID: Disable Face ID with a Mask.
- Choose Reset Face ID to disable Face ID.

You may disable Face ID as an unlock method in the event that your iPhone is misplaced or stolen by enabling the Find My iPhone Lost Mode.

CHAPTER TWO

HOW TO SET UP FACETIME ON IPHONE

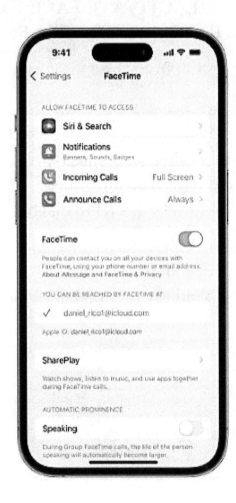

Go to Settings > FaceTime, and then turn it on to begin using FaceTime. Click the "You can be reached by FaceTime at" button and, if prompted, provide your Apple ID or phone number.

CALL SOMEONE USING FACETIME

Launch FaceTime, choose New FaceTime, and then input the contact's name or number to initiate the call. For video calls, use the FaceTime button; for voice calls, tap the Call button (not accessible in all countries or regions). There is a maximum capacity of 32 participants per call.

Making and sending a link to a call using Messages or Mail is a great way to reach someone who doesn't own an Apple device. Start by opening FaceTime and then tapping the Create Link button.

TAKE USE OF FACETIME'S TOOLS

Turn your speaker, camera, and microphone on or off, snap a live photo, and more using the FaceTime controls while you're on a conversation. If the controls aren't visible, tap the screen.

GATHER AROUND TO WATCH, LISTEN, AND PLAY

In order to begin sharing media files or starting a group exercise session while on a FaceTime conversation, go to the FaceTime settings and look for the Share Content option. If you can't find it, touch the screen.

Here are some applications for you to peruse. Collaborate as you listen and play, and then choose one (like TV, Music, or Fitness, for instance).

HOW TO MAKE GROUP FACETIME CALL ON IPHONE

(Not accessible in all countries or areas) The FaceTime app allows you to have group FaceTime conversations with up to 32 people.

ENGAGE IN A GROUP FACETIME MEETING.

- Go to the very top of your FaceTime screen and touch the "New FaceTime" button.
- Input the names or phone numbers of the individuals you want to contact in the top-most input box.

  Alternately, you may access Contacts by tapping the Add Contact icon. Use your call history to get recommended contacts instead.

- To initiate a FaceTime video call or voice call, just touch the FaceTime button.

On the screen, you can see each player as a tile. Tiles are highlighted or made more visible when participants communicate (verbally or via sign language) or when you touch them. At the very bottom, you'll see a row of tiles that don't fit on the screen. Swipe along the row to discover an unseen participant. If a picture isn't available, the participant's initials could be shown on the tile instead.

In the FaceTime settings, locate the Speaking option and toggle it off. This will prevent the tile of the person speaking or signing during a group FaceTime session from being more prominent.

Note That in order for sign language detection to work, the presenter's model must be supported. Furthermore, everyone involved requires an iOS device running iOS 14, iPadOS 14, or macOS 11, or a later version.

LAUNCH A FACETIME MEETING DIRECTLY FROM A GROUP CHAT IN MESSAGES.

Anyone participating in an iMessage group chat may initiate a Group FaceTime session with the rest of the group.

1. In your iMessage chat, in the upper right, you should see the FaceTime button; tap on it.
2. Perform one of these tasks:
   - Choose the audio option for FaceTime.
   - Select FaceTime Video.

INCLUDE A NEW PARTY IN A CALL

At any point during a FaceTime session, either participant has the option to invite another person.

1. If the FaceTime controls aren't already visible, press the screen to bring them up. Then, hit the More Info icon on top of the buttons, and last, tap Add People.
2. Input the desired contact's name, Apple ID, or phone number into the top field.

To import a contact from your phone's address book, use the Add Contact button.

3. Push the Add People button.

ASSIST WITH A GROUP FACETIME MEETING

Anyone may send you an invitation to join a group FaceTime call, and you'll get a notice when it comes in.

END A FACETIME MEETING

Press the Leave button to end a group call whenever you like.

With at least two people still on the line, the call may continue.

HOW TO SHARE YOUR SCREEN IN A FACETIME CALL ON IPHONE

You may share your screen in the FaceTime app to include websites, applications, and more into your conversation—as long as your device fulfills the minimal system requirements. Everyone on the call may see and hear your comments as you ask for criticism on your work, share an album of photos, and more.

SHARE YOUR SCREEN IN A FACETIME CALL

1. If the FaceTime controls aren't accessible while you're on a conversation, press the screen to bring them up. Then, hit the Share Content option.
2. Press the Share My Screen button to broadcast your whole screen.

The Share Content button shows a countdown from 3 to 1, and then a little screen capture appears in the FaceTime conversation. The other people on the call may touch it to make it bigger so they can see what you're showing.

You may end screen sharing by tapping the Share Content icon.

HOW TO USE SHAREPLAY TO WATCH, LISTEN AND PLAY TOGETHER IN FACETIME ON IPHONE

While on a FaceTime chat with loved ones, you may all enjoy your favorite programs, movies, and music simultaneously thanks to SharePlay in the FaceTime app. With synchronized playback and shared controls, you and your call partners can experience a seamless connection in real time. Smart volume allows you to keep chatting while viewing or listening to media by dynamically adjusting the audio. With some titles supported by Game Center, you and your pals may even play multiplayer games while on a FaceTime conversation.

Tip: Launch SharePlay is to hold two iPhones side by side.

During a FaceTime chat, you may also utilize SharePlay in other applications. Press the Share Content option while on the phone, and then scroll down to Apps for SharePlay to view all of the available SharePlay applications.

Note: You may need a membership to use some of the applications that support SharePlay. In order for everyone to enjoy a movie or TV program in one sitting, it is essential that each individual has the necessary resources to access the material. This may be achieved by a subscription or a purchase, and the device must also fulfill certain system requirements. There are certain movies and TV series that SharePlay does not enable sharing internationally. It's possible that not all nations or areas have access to Apple services, including FaceTime and some of its capabilities.

PARTICIPATE IN A FACETIME VIDEO CHAT

During a FaceTime connection, you and your loved ones may watch TV episodes and movies simultaneously.

1. Press the FaceTime button on your iPhone to begin a call.

2. Go to the Share Content section, then choose an app from the list. See, Hear, and Do It All at Once (like the Apple TV app)

   On the other hand, you may access the Home Screen and launch a SharePlay-compatible video streaming app.

3. Pick up a movie or TV program to watch, hit the Play button, and then, if an option appears, choose Play for Everyone to start viewing with everyone on the call. (For others

to be able to see the movie, they may need to touch the Join SharePlay button.)

The video begins playing simultaneously for all participants on the call who have permission to see it. We encourage anyone without access to obtain it (whether that's by paying for a subscription, making a purchase, or taking advantage of a free trial, if offered).

The playback controls allow each viewer to independently adjust the playback speed, pause, rewind, and playback direction. (Closed captioning and loudness are two settings that each user controls independently.)

Keep viewing without disturbing the audio by utilizing Picture in Picture. Use it to place an order, check your email, or even go into Messages to have a text discussion about the video.

DURING A FACETIME CONVERSATION, YOU MAY INVITE YOUR CONTACTS TO SEE A VIDEO FROM A COMPATIBLE APP.

If your iPhone is up to snuff, you may make a FaceTime conversation inside the Apple TV app (or any compatible video app) while you're surfing the web or viewing a movie, and then use SharePlay to synchronize your sharing with others. On each participant's device, the material must be accessible in the same way, whether that's via a subscription or a purchase.

1. Find the program or movie you want to share in the Apple TV app (or another compatible video app), then touch the item to see its information.
2. To access SharePlay, first press the Share icon.
3. After you've entered the people you want to share with in the "To" section, hit the "FaceTime" button.
4. Start or Play will allow you to start utilizing SharePlay when the FaceTime connection connects.

After recipients hit Open, viewing may begin.

Please be informed that those who do not already have a membership may easily become subscribers in order to access this information.

You may start streaming the video to Apple TV once it begins playing.

MIRROR YOUR SHAREPLAY CONTENT ON YOUR APPLE TV.

You can transfer videos from your iPhone to Apple TV so you can view them on a larger screen once you've begun watching them on your iPhone.

Perform one of the following on an iPhone:

* To play content on Apple TV, open the streaming app, find the AirPlay button, and press it.
* Select Apple TV as the playback destination after opening Control Center and tapping the Playback Destination button.

On Apple TV, the video will play in sync, and on your iPhone, you may continue the chat.

JOIN A FACETIME CALL WHILE LISTENING TO MUSIC.

Over a FaceTime chat, you and your friends may jam out to your favorite album or playlist. Listen along, see what's next, add songs to a shared queue, and more on any device that satisfies the minimal system requirements. This includes everyone on the call who has access to the music, whether it's via a subscription, a transaction, or a free trial.

1. Create a group FaceTime meeting.
2. Hit the share button, and then choose an app to listen to music from the list that appears. See, Hear, and Do It All at Once (like the Apple TV app)

On the other hand, you may access the Home Screen and launch a SharePlay-compatible music streaming app, like the Music app, for instance.

3. To start listening to the music together, choose it and then hit the Play button. (Some callers may need to use the Join SharePlay button before they can hear the music.)

All participants on the call with access to the material will hear the music begin playing simultaneously. We encourage anyone without access to obtain it (whether that's by paying for a subscription, making a purchase, or taking advantage of a free trial, if offered).

Each listener has their own set of controls that let them to go forward or backward through the song, rewind, stop, or skip to a specific section. Plus, everyone on the call has the ability to add music to the shared queue.

DURING A FACETIME CHAT, YOU MAY ASK YOUR FRIENDS TO LISTEN TO MUSIC FROM AN APP THAT SUPPORTS GROUP AUDIO.

If your iPhone satisfies the system requirements, you may use SharePlay to synchronize the music playing in the background when you initiate a FaceTime conversation using the Music app or another compatible music app. Everyone may use the play/pause/rewind/scroll controls to go to whatever section of the song they want. In addition, everyone with SharePlay may contribute music to the group's queue. The music must be accessible to the individuals you want to share it with, maybe via a subscription.

1. Launch Apple Music or your preferred music app, then choose the tracks you want to share.
2. Choose an option from these:
   - After selecting the song, hit the More option and then choose SharePlay.
   - Select SharePlay from the menu that appears after tapping the More icon in the upper right.
3. After you've entered the people you want to share with in the "To" section, hit the "FaceTime" button.
4. Tap Start once the FaceTime call establishes a connection.

Hit the song title in the upper right of the FaceTime interface, then hit Open, to start listening. Everyone on the call who can hear the music will hear it start playing simultaneously.

Note: Those who are now unable to view the stuff you provide are kindly requested to do so.

WHILE ON A FACETIME CONVERSATION WITH PALS, USE GAME CENTER TO PLAY SOME GAMES.

In Game Center, you and your friends may play compatible multiplayer games while on a FaceTime conversation. Before you can locate and download a compatible multiplayer game for Game Center from the App Store, you need to add friends to your profile and set it up in Settings.

Launch the game, hit Start SharePlay, and then follow the on-screen prompts while on a FaceTime chat.

HOW TO CHANGE FACETIME VIDEO SETTINGS ON IPHONE

Using the FaceTime app, you can choose between cameras, activate Portrait mode, and turn your camera on or off while you're on a conversation.

PORTRAIT MODE ALLOWS YOU TO BLUR THE BACKDROP.

Just as in the Camera app, you can activate Portrait mode on certain models to make yourself the center of attention by blurring the backdrop.

1. Tap your tile while you're on a FaceTime chat.
2. Press the tile's Blur Background button.
   - Pressing the button twice will disable Portrait mode.

In Control Center, you also have the option to activate Portrait mode. Press the Video Effects button after opening Control Center.

MOVE TO THE BACK CAMERA.

To switch between the front and back cameras when on a FaceTime chat, touch your tile and then choose the option.

Pressing the Flip to Back Camera button one more will return you to the front-facing camera.

Note: That you may touch the screen once to magnify the picture while you're utilizing the back camera. The picture reverts to its original size when you tap it again.

DISABLE THE CAMERA.

To activate the camera while on a FaceTime call, touch the screen to bring up the controls, and then hit the button. (To activate the camera again, tap it once more.)

HOW TO ADJUST THE AUDIO SETTINGS FOR FACETIME ON AN IPHONE

The FaceTime app's Spatial Audio feature makes it seem like your pals are physically there in the room with you. Their voices are dispersed and seem to be emanating from the screen's corresponding characters' directions.

Note: That the following AirPod models (sold separately) are compatible with Spatial Audio: AirPods (3rd generation), AirPods Pro (all models), and AirPods Max.

REMOVE EXTRANEOUS NOISES

On some models, you have the option to activate Voice Isolation mode, which allows you to isolate your voice during FaceTime calls while also filtering out background noise. When you're on a FaceTime conversation, you may isolate your voice by turning on the "Voice Isolation" feature.

Launch Control Center, go to Mic Mode, and finally, choose Voice Isolation when you're on a FaceTime chat.

MAKE USE OF THE AMBIENT NOISES.

When you're on a FaceTime conversation and want everyone around you to hear you, you may use Wide Spectrum mode, which is available on certain models.

To access Wide Spectrum while on a FaceTime chat, launch Control Center, hit Mic Mode, and finally, choose it.

MUTE THE MUSIC

To silence a FaceTime call, press the screen to bring up the controls (if they aren't already visible), and then hit the mute button.

Pressing the button again will activate the sound again.

Your microphone will detect when you're speaking even when the sound is off, and you'll get a notification to let you know that it's muted. By tapping the Mute On button, you can turn it back on.

CHAPTER THREE

IPHONE CAMERA BASICS

Acquire the skill of taking photographs with the iPhone's Camera. Select a shooting mode (Photo, Video, Cinematic, Pano, or Portrait) and adjust the magnification to get the perfect photo.

OPEN CAMERA

Choose one of these options to open Camera:

- Select Camera from the Home Screen of your iPhone.
- To unlock your iPhone, swipe left on the screen.
- On the iPhone's lock screen, press and hold the camera button.
- Launch Control Center and choose the Camera icon.

  To activate the camera, ask Siri to say "Open Camera." Master the art of using Siri.

- Assigning the Action button to launch the Camera is a feature available on the iPhone 15 Pro and iPhone 15 Pro Max. Refer to The Action button on the iPhone 15 Pro and iPhone 15 Pro Max may be used and customized.

To help you keep track of when Camera is active, a green dot will show up in the upper right corner of your screen. Refer to Manage user access to hardware capabilities.

TO SNAP A PICTURE

Open the camera app, then either push the volume buttons or press and hold the shutter button.

NAVIGATE THE VARIOUS SHOOTING MODES

The default mode that appears when you launch Camera is Photo. To capture both static images and moving ones, go to Photo mode. You may switch between several shooting modes by swiping left or right on the screen:

- *Video:* To record a video, go to the section on the subject.
- *Time-Lapse Video:* Make a time-lapse film documenting the passage of time.
- *Slo-mo:* Add a slow-motion effect to your video.
- *Panning:* Take a wide shot of a scene, such as a landscape.
- *Portrait:* Enhance your images with a depth-of-field effect (on compatible devices).
- *Cinematic:* Cinematic movies for adding a depth-of-field effect to your films using compatible models.
- *Square:* Use a square format for taking pictures.

If you're using an iPhone 11 or later, you may choose between 4:3, 16:9, and Square by tapping the Camera Controls button.

ROTATE THE VIEW TO MAGNIFY

- To zoom in or out on any model, use the Camera app and use the screen pinch gesture.
- You may rapidly zoom in or out on iPhone models with Dual or Triple camera systems by switching between 0.5x, 1x, 2x, 2.5x, 3x, or 5x.

The exact numbers vary by model. Hold down the zoom controls while dragging the slider to the right or left for finer zoom control.

HOW TO CHANGE ADVANCED CAMERA SETTINGS ON IPHONE

Find out how to use the advanced capabilities of the camera to take pictures faster, give them a more personalized appearance, and see what's beyond the camera's viewfinder.

MODIFY THE PRIMARY CAMERA'S PIXEL DENSITY

The primary camera of the iPhone 15 comes with a default resolution of 24 megapixels. A variety of megapixels, from 12 to 48, are at your disposal.

To change the photo mode from 12 MP to 24 MP, go to the camera's settings, formats, and photo mode.

To get a resolution of 48 megapixels, activate Resolution Control or ProRAW & Resolution Control (whatever applies to your model) in the Settings menu, then navigate to Camera > Formats.

After activating ProRAW & Resolution Control on the iPhone 15 Pro and iPhone 15 Pro Max, you will be able to choose the default format by tapping Pro Default and then selecting a choice. Launch Camera, and then toggle the selected format on and off using the button on top of the screen. You may choose another format by touching and holding the toggle.

ALTER THE VISIBILITY OF THE WORLD OUTSIDE THE FRAME.

To demonstrate what's possible with an additional lens in the camera system that captures a broader field of vision, the camera preview on compatible models shows material beyond the frame. As a default, View Outside the Frame is set to On.

You may disable View Outside the Frame in the Camera settings by going to the menu and selecting that option.

TOGGLE THE SWITCH FOR PRIORITIZE QUICKER SHOOTING.

You may take more pictures with a faster shutter speed by adjusting the image processing under the Prioritize Faster Shooting option. The default setting is to prioritize faster shooting.

Navigate to Settings > Camera and deselect Prioritize Faster Shooting to disable it.

DISABLE AND RE-ENABLE LENS CORRECTION

Lens Correction is an option on compatible devices that, when turned on, makes front- or ultra-wide-angle shots seem more realistic. By default, Lens Correction is enabled.

Navigate to Settings > Camera and deselect Lens Correction to disable it.

ALTER THE STATE OF SCENE DETECTION

The Scene Detection feature, available on iPhone 12 models, can detect the subject of your shot and apply a customized filter to enhance its best features. Preset Scene Detection is set to On.

Navigate to Settings > Camera and deselect Scene Detection to disable it.

HOW TO APPLY PHOTOGRAPHIC STYLES WITH YOUR IPHONE CAMERA

You may change the way Camera takes pictures by applying a Photographic Style on devices that support it. Rich Contrast, Vibrant, Warm, and Cool are the default styles to choose from; you may further personalize them by modifying the warmth and tone settings. With each shot taken in Photo mode, the camera will remember your preference.

Right in Camera, you have the ability to modify and adapt photographic styles.

PICK A PHOTOGRAPHY APPROACH

By default, your iPhone's camera is set to Standard, a neutral mode that captures accurate images. What follows is an example of how to change your photographic style:

1. Press the Camera Controls button after opening the Camera app.
2. Select a style from the list by tapping the Photographic Styles icon and swiping left:
   - A dramatic effect is achieved by using deeper shadows, richer hues, and more contrast.
   - Colors that are both very bright and vibrant provide an appearance that is both striking and organic.
   - To make it seem cozier, golden undertones are used.
   - Classy: A outfit with blue undertones is classy.

If you want to change the look of your photos, you can do that by tapping the Tone and Warmth sliders that are located underneath the frame and dragging them to the left or right. To restore the default settings, use the Reset button next to Photographic Styles.

3. To use the Photographic Style, press the corresponding button.

Select the Photographic Styles On button in the upper-right corner of the screen to modify or alter an existing Photographic Style. By selecting Standard from the style options, you may end the use of a Photographic Style.

The Settings menu also allows you to alter the Photographic Styles: Enter the following menu: Settings > Camera > Photographic Styles.

HOW TO USE YOUR IPHONE'S CAMERA TO CAPTURE LIVE PHOTOS.

Take live photos with your iPhone's camera. You may record the audio and everything that occurs just before and after you snap a picture with a Live Photo. Taking a Live snapshot is quite similar to taking any other kind of snapshot.

1. Launch the camera.
2. Turn on Live Photo and make sure the Camera is in Photo mode.

The Live Photo button will show up at the top of the camera screen when Live Photo is turned on. If the Live Photo button is slashed, it indicates that the function is disabled. To activate or deactivate Live Photo, just tap the button.

3. To capture a Live Photo, just press the Shutter button.
4. Touch and hold the screen to play the Live Photo after tapping the photo thumbnail at the bottom of the screen.

CHAPTER FOUR

HOW TO CUSTOMIZE IPHONE LIVE PHOTOS

Live Photos, the main photo, and entertaining effects like Bounce and Loop are all editable in the Photos app.

MODIFY PHOTOS IN REAL-TIME

You can edit a Live Photo using the standard iPhone tools, but you can also alter the key photo, shorten the duration, silence the music, and convert it to a still image.

1. Launch the Picture app on your iOS device.
2. Launch Live Photos and hit the Edit button.
3. Select an action by tapping the Live Photo button:
   - After repositioning the white frame in the viewer, choose "Make Key Photo" and then "Done" to set the photo as the main image.
   - To crop a live photo, just drag the frame viewer's edges to choose the frames you want to use.

- Create a static image: To disable the Live function, tap the Live button located at the top of the screen. The Live picture turns into a static image of the featured picture.
- To make a live photo unviewable, look for the "Mute" button at the screen's top. To remove the mute option, press the button again.

Note: That if you alter the key picture in a Live picture produced with a portrait effect on an iPhone 15 model, the portrait effect will be lost.

PERSONALIZE A LIVE PHOTO WITH EFFECTS

Live Photos may be transformed into entertaining films with the addition of effects.

1. Launch the Picture app on your iOS device.
2. View a Live Image.
3. To access the live photo feature, go to the top left and tap the Live button. From there, choose an option:
   - In a live setting, the video playback function is activated.
   - Loop: The video will play back the same scene indefinitely.

- With a bounce, you can go ahead and backward in time.
- Long Exposure: Blurs moving objects to mimic the look of a DSLR's long exposure mode.
- Live Off: Disables the ability to watch live video or apply effects while playing back video.

HOW TO TAKE BURST PHOTOS ON IPHONE

The iPhone's camera app has a burst mode that lets you snap 10 shots in a row for a certain amount of seconds. Use this function to get a shot of a moving subject or to make sure you get a good one.

1. Launch the Camera app.

2. To the left, swipe the shutter button. To stop, raise your finger.

3. Then, touch the thumbnail of a picture to choose it for storage.

4. Press the Choose button.

5. Though the gray dots indicate recommended photographs, you are free to retain whatever ones you choose.

6. Select all of the images you want to save by tapping the circle in the bottom right corner.

96

7. Hit the Finish button.

8. You'll have the option to save all your photographs or only the ones you choose.

HOW TO SNAP A SELFIE WITH THE CAMERA ON YOUR IPHONE.

To capture a selfie, use the camera. There are three modes available for taking selfies: photo, portrait, and video.

1. Bring up the iPhone camera.
2. To activate the front-facing camera, press the Back-Facing button on the Camera Chooser.
3. Keep your iPhone held aloft.

   Use the in-frame arrows as a pointer to expand the view.

4. To start recording or snap a picture, press the volume buttons or press and hold the shutter button.

Go to Settings > Camera and toggle on Mirror Front Camera to shoot a selfie without inverting the image; instead, it will record the photo as it appears in the front-facing camera frame.

HOW TO USE NIGHT MODE ON YOUR IPHONE

When the camera detects low light, you may utilize Night mode on compatible iPhone models to take images.

On iPhones released in 2011 and after, you'll find the Night mode.

USE NIGHT MODE TO CAPTURE IMAGES IN DIM LIGHT.

The camera will switch to night mode automatically if it senses that the light level is too low. While using Night mode, the top-most icon that says "No alt supplied for Image" will become yellow. Whether your iPhone takes a few seconds or a few seconds at the most to capture a shot in Night mode depends on how dark the environment is. Your exposure setting is also adjustable.

Retain your iPhone stable throughout the whole capture process for the finest outcomes. If you're having trouble keeping your iPhone steady when taking photos, try setting it on a sturdy surface or using a tripod.

If your iPhone senses motion while you're taking a picture, you may use the crosshairs to stabilize the photograph on iOS 14 and later. Simply press the stop button underneath the slider to halt a Night mode shot mid-take instead than waiting for the capture to complete.

VARY THE DURATION OF THE CAPTURE

A timer shows up next to the Night mode symbol when you press the shutter button to tell you how long the photograph will take in Night mode.

Use the up arrow next to the viewfinder to experiment with longer Night mode shots. Select Max from the slider above the shutter button to prolong the recording duration, then tap the Night mode button that shows below the viewfinder. The slider doubles as a timer that displays the remaining amount of time till the shot is taken.

USE THE NIGHTTIME SELFIE MODE

- Launch the Camera app.
- Crank up the front-facing camera by pressing the button.
- Keep your iPhone held aloft.
- Document the moment with a selfie.

Note: You may take selfies in night mode on the following iPhone models: 15, 15, Plus, 15 Pro, 15 Pro Max, 14, 14 Pro, 14 Pro Max, 13, iPhone 13, mini, 13 Pro, 13 Pro Max, 12, iPhone 12 mini, 12 Pro, and 12 Pro Max.

SEIZE THE NIGHT FILMING IN SLOW MOTION

Using a tripod and the Night mode Time-lapse feature, you may record films with longer interval frames even in dim lighting. To use the Time-lapse feature, launch the Camera app and slide left. Press and hold the shutter buttonImage does not have an alternative that may be used to record your video.

Note: All of the following iPhone models: 15, 15, Plus, 15 Pro, 15 Pro Max, 14, 14 Plus, 14 Pro, 14 Pro Max, 13, 13 mini, 13 Pro, 13 Pro Max, 12, 12 mini, 12 Pro, and 12 Pro Max, as well as the following: iPhone 13, iPhone 13, Pro, 13 Pro Max, iPhone 12, and iPhone 13 mini.

MAKE USE OF PORTRAIT NIGHT MODE

- To access Portrait mode, launch the Camera app and slide left.
- Use the on-screen instructions as a guide.
- Press and hold the shutter buttonImage does not have an alternative.

Note: Various iPhone models, including the 15 Pro, 15 Pro Max, 14 Pro, 13 Pro, 12 Pro, and 12 Pro Max, have Night mode Portrait.

ALLOW LIVE PHOTO CAPTURE AND FLASH

You can't use Live Photos or the flash when your iPhone is in Night mode. Manual activation of these functionalities is possible. If you want to use Live Photos or the flash, you'll have to disable Night mode first.

In low-light settings, the flash will activate automatically if set to Auto. Press the arrow next to "No alt supplied for Image" in the viewfinder to manually activate Flash. Choose "On" after tapping the Flash button (no other image is provided) that shows below the viewfinder.

CHAPTER FIVE

HOW TO CHANGE THE ORIENTATION OF PANORAMA MODE

1. Start up your iOS device's Camera app.
2. Press and hold to enter PANO mode.
3. You may snap panoramic images in either a left or right direction by tapping the arrow button or wherever on the panoramic strip. Return to the normal left-to-right panning by tapping it once more.
4. Pressing the shutter button will now take a panoramic.

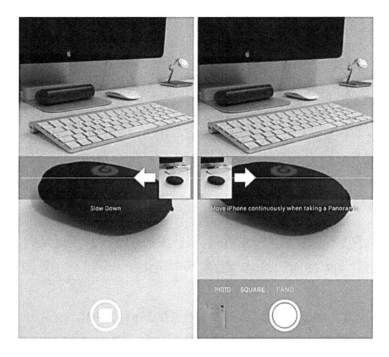

Vertical Panoramic Shots Are Also Within Your Capabilities.

You may already be used to photographing panoramas from left to right, and now you can do the same from right to left. In case you were unaware, you can also shoot vertical panorama shots by gently moving your phone vertically (from bottom to top) in landscape mode after opening the Camera app and switching to PANO mode. Just press the arrow or the strip to adjust its direction (upwards or downwards).

HOW TO USE THE IPHONE CAMERA TO GET CLOSE-UP SHOTS AND MOVIES OF OBJECTS.

Stunning, in-focus macro photography is captured by Camera using the Ultra Wide camera on compatible devices. Macro, Live Photo, and slow-motion/time-lapse video capture capabilities are all at your fingertips.

CAPTURE A CLOSE-UP SHOT OR FOOTAGE

1. To take a picture or video with your iPhone, open the Camera app.
2. Close your distance to the topic to no more than two cm. The Ultra Wide lens will be activated mechanically.
3. Use the shutter button to snap a picture, or press and hold the record button to begin and end video recording.

THE USE OF TIME-LAPSE OR MACRO SLOW-MOTION PHOTOGRAPHY

1. Get your iPhone's Camera app and go to the Slo-mo or Time-lapse settings.
2. Press the.5x button to activate the Ultra Wide camera, and then approach the subject up close.
3. To begin and end recording, just tap the Record button.

MANAGE THE AUTOMATIC SWITCHING OF MACROS

If you want to take macro shots or record movies, you may set the camera to switch to the Ultra Wide lens at a certain time.

1. Get up close to your subject and open up the Camera app on your iPhone.

   The Auto Macro On button will show up on the screen as soon as you approach your subject at macro distance.

2. Disabling automatic macro switching is as simple as tapping the Auto Macro On button.

   Hint: you may tap or back up if the picture or video becomes fuzzy.Press 5x to activate the Ultra Wide lens.

3. To activate automatic macro switching again, tap the Auto Macro Off button.

Go to the Settings menu, then choose Camera. From there, disable Macro Control to prevent the camera from automatically switching to the Ultra Wide lens whenever you take a macro shot or video.

You may enable Macro Control under Settings > Camera > Preserve Settings if you'd want your

Macro Control settings to be saved across camera sessions.

WHAT IS PRORAW ON IPHONE

In most cases, saving a picture in RAW format prevents processing before saving, giving you more room to manoeuvre in post-production. While preserving the ability to modify aspects like exposure, sharpness, color, and more, Apple's ProRAW combines data from the RAW format with the picture processing capabilities of the iPhone.

The format is similar to picture formats such as JPEG, PNG, HEIC, and others. The iPhone 12 Pro, subsequent Pro models, and the 15-series all support ProRAW. Images saved in ProRAW format will be more substantial in size compared to other picture formats such as JPEG and PNG.

Note: If you're using an iPhone model other than the 15 series, the ProRAW picture size may easily exceed 100MB. Use this functionality sparingly, if at all. File sizes remain about 5MB thanks to the new HEIF Max format used by the iPhone 15 series.

Taking 48MP photographs in ProRAW format is possible on the iPhone 15 and iPhone 14 Pro series, which you should know now that you have comprehended ProRAW. Follow these steps to get the most of your iPhone's 48MP camera:

HOW TO ENABLE 48MP PRORAW PHOTOS ON IPHONE

1. Launch the iPhone's Settings app.
2. To access the camera, scroll down and choose it.
3. Select the Formats menu item.
4. Toggle the switch that says "ProRAW" next to "Resolution Control" (or "Resolution Control" on older iPhones).

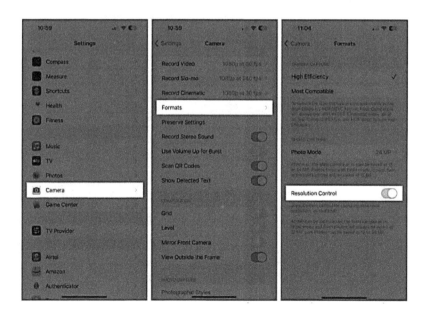

- On the iPhone 14 Pro, 15 Pro, and 15 Pro Max, go to the Settings > General > Default > HEIF Max or ProMAX (up to 48MP).

5. To access the iPhone camera, launch the app. Verify that the HEIF MAX or RAW MAX displays are turned on and not hidden.

6. Do not change the focus length from 1x.

7. Press the shutter button to take the picture.

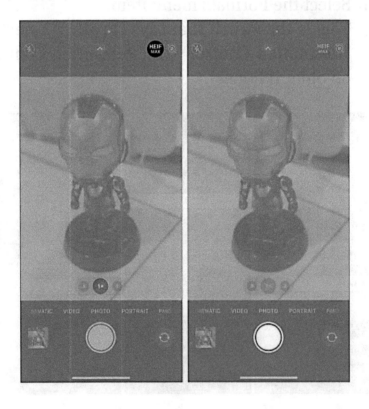

Choose between high and raw modes by pressing and holding the corresponding button. Additionally, you have the option to capture 48MP photos via Halide or another third-party program.

HOW TO EDIT AND SHARE APPLE PRORAW PHOTOS

The RAW files are saved in the industry-standard DNG format. In order to make changes to the picture later, save it with the.dig extension. Any third-party RAW picture editing program that supports the.dng format, as well as the iPhone Photos app, may edit them. Lightroom is my go-to because of all the professional tools it provides for customizing the picture to my liking.

Some of the best programs for working with ProRAW images are these:

❖ Lightroom
❖ Adobe
❖ Photoshop
❖ Snapseed

You may also use the.jpg extension to share Apple Photos ProRAW photographs. It is partially compressed to a.jpeg format, thus its appearance may vary from what you were expecting. Using AirDrop or iCloud, you may export these photographs to the Apple Ecosystem.

HOW TO ENABLE AND DISABLE HDR ON IPHONE

High Dynamic Range (HDR) photography is standard on all iPhones released in 2018 and after. We can access it under the Photos app's settings on your iPhone. To See Full HDR, Select This Option, and the Display Will Automatically Adjust to Display the Full Dynamic Range of Your Photos.

1. Great photos may be seen by enabling the option in the Settings app, then going to Photos, and finally, View Full HDR.

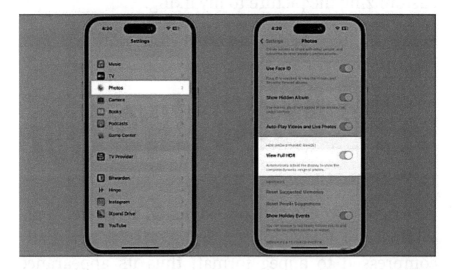

2. Unfortunately, the latest iPhone models (iPhone 12 and above) allow us to disable smart HDR for videos. as this guide explains.

Models Prior To iPhone 11,

1. Launch the iPhone's Settings app.

2. Scroll down and press hit the camera.

Turn on the "HDR" option that you'll see under the "HDR" area. All the way up to the iPhone 11 series.

High dynamic range (HDR) cleverly merges the finest elements of many exposures into one. Put the HDR version side by side with the conventionally exposed shot.

Top Priority!

Smart HDR Is Now Activated By Default On All New iPhones (12, 13, 14, and 15).

Your camera app will be able to toggle HDR on and off, as well as between automatic and off, after you activate it.

- On: High dynamic range photography is always enabled.
- Off: Disable HDR picture quality automatically

- Without user intervention: your iPhone can sense its environment and activate or deactivate the camera app based on that.

TURN ON OR OFF HDR VIDEO ON AN IPHONE

If you own an iPhone 12 or later model, you can find the options to enable or disable HRD Video recording here. Dolby Vision HDR, which improves contrast and color accuracy, is an optional feature that your iPhone may use while recording video.

- Turn on "HDR Video" in your iPhone's Settings app by going to the Camera > Record Video menu.

Quicktime movie marked as High Dynamic Range in the Photos app,

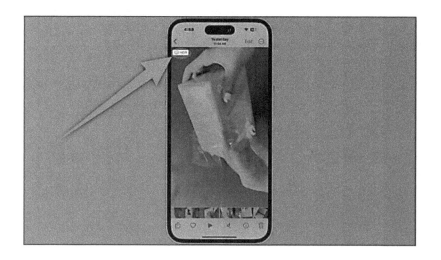

ENABLE OR DISABLE HDR ON THE IPHONE.

It is possible to disable HDR photo quality on the camera without going into the settings.

On the iPhone, we have the ability to temporarily deactivate the HDR camera.

1. Launch the Camera app on your iPhone. 4. You may easily turn HDR off by tapping on the corresponding option.
2. Go to Settings > Camera > Record Video to disable HDR on your iPhone. After that, disable HDR and leave it that way.

CHAPTER SIX

HOW TO USE YOUR IPHONE'S CAMERA TO CAPTURE VIDEOS.

The iPhone's Camera app allows you to capture both regular video and QuickTime movies. Master the art of switching between shooting modes to capture time-lapse, slow-motion, and cinematic footage.

Note: that video recording is not an option while using FaceTime or a phone call.

RECORD A VIDEO

1. To switch between camera modes, open Camera and then choose Video mode.
2. Start recording by tapping the Record button or pressing the volume buttons. You have the option to perform the following when recording:
   o The white Shutter button may be used to capture a static image.
   o Zoom in and out by pinching the screen.
   o Touch and hold the 1x button, then move the slider (for models that support it) to get a closer look.

3. To end recording, either tap the Record button or push the volume buttons simultaneously.

Note: A green dot will display at the top of the screen whenever Camera is in use for your security.

CAPTURE ULTRA-HIGH DEFINITION OR 4K FOOTAGE.

There are a variety of high-quality video formats that may be recorded on iPhones, including HD, 4K, HD (PAL), and 4K (PAL).

Press the Record Video button after going to Settings > Camera.

Choose a video format and frame rate that work with your iPhone.

Note: Video files will grow in size as the frame rate and quality increase.

Please take note that many nations and areas in South America, Asia, Africa, and Europe use the PAL television visual format.

MAKE USE OF ACTION MODE.

When using Video mode for filming, Action mode on iPhone 14 and iPhone 15 devices offers better stabilization. To activate Action mode, tap the button located at the top of the screen. To deactivate it, tap the same button.

Take Note: In strong light, action mode performs at its finest. Go to the Settings menu, then touch Camera. From there, choose Record Video. Finally, enable Action Mode Lower Light if you want to utilize Action mode in low light. The highest possible resolution for action mode captures is 2.8K.

CAPTURE A VIDEO WITH QUICKTAKE

Recordings made in QuickTime's Photo mode are called QuickTake videos. Locking the Record button allows you to continue snapping still photographs even as you record a QuickTake movie.

1. Launch QuickTake by opening the Camera app and then pressing and holding the Shutter button.

2. To record without using your hands, slide the shutter button to the right and release it when you see the lock.

- You may capture a still image while recording by tapping the Shutter button, which is located below the frame.
- If you want to go closer to your subject while filming without using your hands, you may swipe up or squeeze out on the screen.

3. To end recording, press the Record button.

Hint: To begin recording a QuickTake video in Photo mode, press and hold the volume up or down button.

In order to see the QuickTake movie on the Photos app, tap on the thumbnail.

CAPTURE A VIDEO IN SLOW MOTION.

Even when your video records normally in slow-motion mode, when you play it back, it will seem to have a slow-motion effect. Another option is to use video editing tools to set a start and end time for the slow-motion effect.

1. Go to the camera and choose the slow-motion option.

   To capture slow-motion footage with the front-facing camera, press the Camera Chooser Back-Facing button on iPhone 11, 12, 13, 14, and 15 models.

2. Start recording by tapping the Record button or pressing the volume buttons.

   To capture a still image while recording, just press the Shutter button.

3. To end recording, either tap the Record button or push the volume buttons simultaneously.

By tapping the video thumbnail and then tapping Edit, you may adjust the speed of playback to slow motion while leaving the remainder of the movie at standard speed. To set the frame viewer to play in slow motion, drag the vertical bars underneath it.

The resolution and frame rate of the slow motion may be adjusted to suit your model. Press Record Slo-mo after going to Settings > Camera to adjust the slow-motion recording options.

As you record, you may easily change the video's resolution and frame rate using the quick toggles.

RECORD A TIME-LAPSE FOOTAGE.

To make a time-lapse film of an event that happens over a period of time, such the sun setting or traffic moving, record footage at certain intervals.

1. Go to the camera's menu and choose the time-lapse option.
2. Position your iPhone so that it can capture a moving scene.
3. If you want to start or stop recording, just hit the Record button.

Tip: A tripod will allow you to film time-lapse recordings with more resolution and brightness in low-light conditions on iPhone 12 models and later.

HOW TO RECORD SPATIAL VIDEOS FOR APPLE VISION PRO WITH YOUR IPHONE CAMERA

The Photos app on Apple Vision Pro allows you to recreate the experiences in three dimensions. Use the Camera on the iPhone 15 Pro and iPhone 15 Pro Max to make spatial films. Any other Apple device can play spatial films in two dimensions, and you may share them just like any other video. These spatial films were shot in SDR at 1080p 30 frames per second. Compared to standard 1080p 30 fps video, which takes about 65 MB per minute, spatial video takes around 130 MB.

Note: If you have an iPhone 15 Pro or 15 Pro Max running iOS 17.2 or later, you may capture videos in three dimensions.

DOCUMENT AERIAL FOOTAGE
1. The camera app on the iPhone 15 Pro and iPhone 15 Pro Max must be open.
2. After you switch to video mode, turn your iPhone so it's facing landscape.

3. To begin recording, press either the volume up or down button, or hit the Record button after turning off the spatial video. While recording, keep these things in mind for optimal results:
   - Rest your iPhone firmly on a flat surface.
   - Use a distance of three to eight feet to frame your subjects.
   - Opt for well-lit, bright lighting.
4. To end recording, either tap the Record button or push the volume buttons simultaneously.
5. To disable spatial video recording, press the Spatial Video On button.

HOW TO SCREEN RECORD ON APPLE IPHONE

1. Before anything else, we have to make sure that our iPhone 15 Pro Max is set to record screen. Step 5 may be skipped if it is already enabled. On the main screen of our Apple iPhone 15 Pro Max, we can see the "Settings" program, which is symbolized by a gear icon. We may use this app to check.

2. Locate the "Control Centre" area in the left-hand menu of the iOS settings icon, and then to click on "Customize controls."

3. Rearrange the order of the controls by clicking and dragging the three horizontal lines to the right of each control. If the screen recording control is already enabled, it will be in the first list we see in the "INCLUDE" section on our iPhone 15 Pro Max. Another option is to use the red button on the left to remove the control.

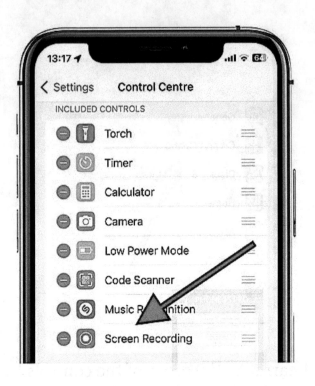

4. If the control isn't already there, find it in the "MORE CONTROLS" section and add it to the panel by clicking the green plus sign. We may now leave the Apple iPhone 15 Pro Max's settings menu after this is finished.

Magnifier

Notes

Quick Not

Screen Recording

Sound Recognition

Stopwatch

Text Size

Voice Memos

Wallet

5. (iPhone 7 and older, iPad running iOS 11 or older) Swipe up from the bottom of the screen where you want to begin the video. (iOS 12 or later on an iPad, iPhone X, or iPad) Swipe down from the top right corner of the screen where you want to begin the video.

6. Press the recording icon on your Apple iPhone 15 Pro Max to start recording a video without using the microphone. A 3-second countdown will start after that, and then the recording will start. A red line and the word "Recording" will appear at the top of the screen, indicating that everything on the screen is being recorded.

You can record audio and video from the microphone on the Apple iPhone 15 Pro Max. To do this, press and hold the Record screen icon. Then, toggle the microphone on and off. Finally, press "Start recording." A 3-second countdown will start, and then the recording will start. This is useful for things like explaining how an app works to a friend or recording a message while the video is playing on the screen.

7. You have two options for stopping recording: Either access the Control Centre and hit the Recording screen icon or press "Stop" on the red line in the top status bar.

8. When you record screen on your Apple iPhone 15 Pro Max, a notice will go up at the top of the screen telling you that the video has been saved to "Photos" (the old name for the Camera Roll).

You may see and share the screen recording you made on your Apple iPhone 15 Pro Max by going to the Photos app and finding it in the bottom left corner.

HOW TO READ QR CODE ON IPHONE

1. Using the built-in "Camera" software, which can be found on the main screen of the Apple iPhone 15 Pro Max, you may scan or capture QR codes.

2. From the Apple iPhone 15 Pro Max camera application, we make sure that we are using the 48 MP, f/1.8, 24mm (wide), 1/1.28", 1.22µm, dual pixel PDAF, sensor-shift OIS 12 MP, f/2.8, 120mm (periscope telephoto), 1.12µm, dual pixel PDAF, 3D sensor-shift OIS, 5x optical zoom 12 MP, f/2.2, 13mm, 120° (ultrawide), 1/2.55", 1.4µm, dual pixel PDAF TOF 3D LiDAR scanner (depth) rear camera and point it at the QR code that we want to read trying to make it appear correctly focused and content within the yellow square or at

least within the viewing space , that is, we cannot bring the camera too close to avoid the code being cut off.

Since there is no "up" or "down" component to the QR code, it makes no difference from whichever angle we approach it from as long as the whole code can be viewed on the screen of the Apple iPhone 15 Pro Max.

3. A notification will pop up on the top of the screen of the Apple iPhone 15 Pro Max to let us know that it has read the QR code and will ask us what to do next. Since most QR codes contain a web address, it will suggest opening "Safari" or the default web browser on our device.

For the notice to open the website or carry out the action, we click on it.

SNAP A PICTURE OF THE QR CODE USING THE COMMAND CENTER

An alternative to using the camera app is a shortcut on the Apple iPhone 15 Pro Max's control center that allows you to access the QR code reader.

1. To access the Apple iPhone 15 Pro Max's control center, swipe down from the top center or right side of the screen.

2. Here you can find the control center of the iPhone 15 Pro Max, where you can find

shortcuts to settings like Wi-Fi, Bluetooth, lock rotation, and more. Find the symbol that looks like a QR code scanner in the picture below.

CHAPTER SEVEN

HOW TO USE CINEMATIC MODE ON IPHONE

First things first:

- Update to iOS 16 or later on your iPhone 15 Pro Max.
- You may choose between 1080p HD at 24, 30, or 60 fps, or 4K HDR at 24 or 30 fps, while using cinematic mode.

Launch the Picture app:

1. Use the right swipe from the lock screen or the home screen to open the Camera app.

Pinch to zoom in on the action:

2. Locate Cinematic by swiping the shooting mode option located at the screen's base.

Craft your photograph:

3. Use the viewfinder of your camera to frame your subject or subjects. Also, bear in mind that three or two persons are the sweet spot for Cinematic mode.

Adjust the depth of field and focus:

4. When the camera is in focus, a yellow box will show up around the object. To manually switch the attention to another topic, just touch the screen.

5. Depending on how far away your subjects are from the backdrop, the camera will automatically alter the depth of field effect, also known as the degree of blurring the background. The depth of field effect may also be fine-tuned manually using the f-number slider located on the left side of the screen.

Recording may begin:

6. You may begin recording your video by tapping the red record button.

7. When individuals enter and exit the frame while recording, the focus will mechanically switch between them. Alternately, you may shift the focus by tapping on the topic itself.

End recording:

8. Repeat the process of tapping the red record button to end recording.

Customize your video in Cinematic mode:

9. Editing a Cinematic mode movie after recording allows you to change the depth of

field effect and focus points. Launch the Photos app, choose the film you want to edit in Cinematic mode, and then hit Edit.

10.   Locate the Cinematic button on the screen's bottom and press on it.

11.   To change the focus point to a certain area in the video, simply tap on it. To tweak the DOF effect, you may also use the f-number slider.

12.   Press the Done button after you're through editing.

SOME FURTHER ADVICE ON HOW TO USE CINEMATIC MODE

o Opt for well-lit areas. Lighting is key while using cinematic mode.

o Maintain a steady iPhone. Keep your iPhone steady or use a tripod if you're shooting in cinematic mode; it's sensitive to motion.

o Keep an eye on the backdrop. Make sure the backdrop isn't very cluttered or obtrusive before using the Cinematic mode's background blur to highlight your subject(s).

o Try out various shifts in emphasis. Focus shifts between subjects may be made to seem quite natural when using the cinematic style. To see how the emphasis changes, try touching on several topics.

HOW TO ORGANIZE YOUR IPHONE'S PICTURE LIBRARY USING ALBUMS.

To browse and arrange your media library, use the Albums feature in the Photos app. You may sort your media library by albums, which include films, portraits, and slow-motion, among others. In the Places album, your images are laid out on a global map, and in the People album, you may peruse your photos according to the people in them.

Your full picture library is shown in the Recents album in the order you uploaded them, while the Favorites album displays the media you tagged as favorites.

Tap to create a new album or folder.

Albums created with iCloud Photos are saved in iCloud. They are current and available on all of your devices as long as you're using the same Apple ID.

CREATE A NEW ALBUM

1. Press the Albums icon located at the screen's base.

2. After tapping the Add button, choose New Album.

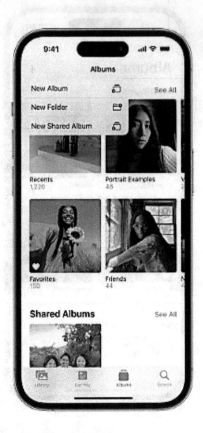

3. Pick an album name and hit the Save button.
4. To add media files to an album, touch the thumbnails of the images and videos you want to use, and then press Add.

PUT A MEDIA FILE FROM YOUR COLLECTION INTO A PICTURE ALBUM.

1. After selecting a picture or video from Library, open it in full screen mode and then choose the More Options option.
2. Select an option from the list after tapping Add to Album:
   - Beginning an album: To create an album, choose New Album and then name it.
   - Enhance a current album: Below My Albums, tap on an existing album.

MAKE AN ALBUM WITH SEVERAL MEDIA FILES BY SELECTING THEM ALL FROM YOUR COLLECTION.

1. Click on Library, and then choose Days or All Photos.
2. Choose the media you want to include by tapping their thumbnails in the Select menu at the top of the screen. Then, find and touch the More Options option.
3. Select an option from the list after tapping Add to Album:
   - Beginning an album: To create an album, choose New Album and then name it.
   - Enhance a current album: Below My Albums, tap on an existing album.

RENAME AN ALBUM

Any album you create in Photos may have its name changed.

1. Select the album you want to change the name of by tapping on Albums.
2. After that, choose More and then touch on Rename Album.
3. After you've entered the new name, hit the Save button.

CHAPTER EIGHT

HOW TO USE LIVE TEXT WITH YOUR IPHONE CAMERA

For text that appears inside the camera frame, you may copy, share, look it up, and translate it. Based on the text that displays in the picture, the camera also offers rapid options to contact phone numbers, browse websites, convert currencies, and more.

1. Launch the camera app on your iPhone and move it to a spot where you can see the text well.
2. Tap the Detect Text button once the yellow frame surrounding the discovered text appears. Then, perform one of these:
   - You may copy and paste content into other apps like Notes or Messages by using the copy function.
   - Pick all All the text within the frame may be selected.
   - Aim High: Display tailored online recommendations.
   - This is a translation service.
   - Look it up online: Research the chosen passage online.

- Text sharing options include AirDrop, Messages, Mail, and more.

Note: You may also utilize the grab points to pick particular text after touching and holding it, allowing you to conduct the tasks mentioned above.

You may make a phone call, go to a website, start an email, change currencies, and more by tapping a fast action at the screen's bottom.

3. To get back to the camera, press the Selected Detect Text button.

Navigate to Settings > Camera on your iPhone, and then disable Show Detected Text to disable Live Text.

HOW TO USE LIVE TEXT TO INTERACT WITH CONTENT IN A PHOTO OR VIDEO ON IPHONE

You can interact with text and information inside images in various ways with Live Text, which is available when you browse photos or stop videos in the Photos app. Use fast actions to do things like make a phone call, launch a webpage, or convert currencies, or choose text to copy, share, or translate.

On compatible devices, you may access Live Text in a variety of apps and features, including Safari, Camera, Quick Look, and more.

TURN ON LIVE TEXT

Please ensure that all available languages have Live Text enabled before you begin using it.

1. Press on Language & Region in the Settings menu.
2. Get Live Text going (green light is on).

EXTRACT, TRANSLATE, AND SEARCH FOR TEXT INSIDE AN IMAGE OR VIDEO

1. Launch an image or stop a movie with text in it.
2. After you've chosen some text, tap and hold it before tapping the Detect Text button.
3. Pick out some text using the grab points, and then do something with it:
   - You may copy and paste text into other apps like Notes or Messages by using the Copy Text feature.
   - Pick all All the text within the frame may be selected.
   - Aim High: Display tailored online recommendations.
   - This is a translation service.
   - Look it up online: Research the chosen passage online.
   - Text sharing options include AirDrop, Messages, Mail, and more.
4. Get back to the video or picture by tapping the Selected Detect Text button.

USE SIMPLE GESTURES TO DO ACTIVITIES WITHIN A VIDEO OR PICTURE.

You may make a phone call, get directions, translate languages, exchange currencies, and more by tapping a fast action at the bottom of the screen, depending on the content of the picture or video.

1. Pause a movie with text in it or access a picture with text in the Photos app.
2. Use the Detect Text button.
3. Select a shortcut at the screen's base by tapping on it.
4. Get back to the video or picture by tapping the Selected Detect Text button.

CHAPTER NINE

TIPS AND TRICKS

1. How To Check The iPhone Battery Cycle

The new battery health indicator is available on all four iPhone 15 models, so you can see when it's time to replace your battery. You no longer need to depend on a third-party program to find out how many charge cycles a battery has before it starts to deteriorate; now you can do it directly.

Navigate to the following: settings > general > about. Locate the section on batteries and verify the value next to "cycle count" by scrolling down.

The number of full charging cycles that your battery has experienced is shown by the "cycle count" indicator. Whether it's all at once or spread out over several days, a charge cycle occurs whenever the battery's power is used up.

2. Steps To Prevent The iPhone 15 Battery From Charging Over 80%

Although seeing the remaining battery life is helpful, the actual benefits are found in the battery health settings.

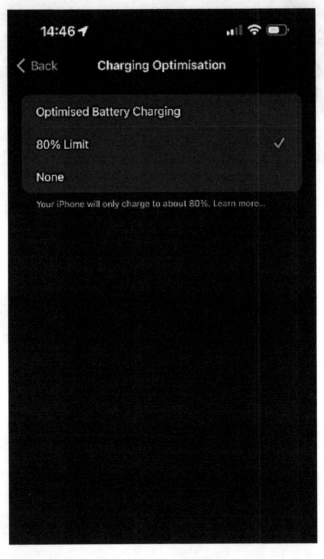

The "optimised" charging mode shortens the time it takes for your iPhone to get from completely charged to fully operational by default on iOS devices. Nevertheless, there is a special function available to iPhone 15 owners that limits the charging limit at 80%.

Battery Health and Charging may be enabled in the settings menu under the battery section. Go ahead and choose the 80% limit when you touch on charge optimization.

3. How To Use Your iPhone To Charge An Apple Watch Or Airpods

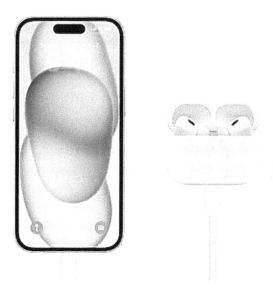

The USB-C connector located on the underside of your iPhone 15 serves many purposes. Not only can you charge other Apple devices with it, but you can also borrow chargers from friends and family without wondering whether they will work.

Use the USB-C cable that came with your iPhone 15 to charge other devices; just connect your phone to one end of the cable and another device, such as another iPhone 15, the brand new AirPods Pro 2, or a charging puck for your Apple Watch that uses the same standard. Not only is it far more handy than the old Lightning charger, but it's also very simple.

4. What Is The Function Of The Dynamic Island?

The pill-shaped notch at the top of your iPhone screen may be confusing if you're coming from an earlier model.

The "Dynamic Island," as it is affectionately known by Apple, first debuted on the iPhone 14 Pro and is now accessible on every iPhone 15 model. App information and interactive alerts, such as low battery warnings, the next direction in Maps, and music controls, are shown in the redesigned notch. Another feature of the Dynamic Island is the ability to launch background applications.

Unfortunately, the only method to hide the cutout and accompanying alerts is to swipe them away. The Dynamic Island can't be disabled at the moment, so you'll have to come to terms with it.

5. Methods For Transforming Landscape Images Into Portrait Mode

You may be familiar with portrait mode if you have taken a picture with your phone during the last few years. Bokeh is a visual effect that uses an out-of-focus, blurry backdrop to highlight the subject of a photograph. Your children, pets, or loved ones will look adorable in these photos.

As a first for iPhones, the newest models allow users to edit images in portrait mode after taking them.

This manner, you can avoid fumbling with the effect controls and missing the crucial shot. Whenever you touch to focus or there's a human, dog, or cat in the frame, the iPhone 15 automatically records depth information, allowing it to accomplish this.

In order to change your landscape mode photos into portrait modes, follow these steps: To add a visual effect to an existing picture in the Photos app, just choose it. If the depth data was preserved, you may activate portrait mode by touching the portrait icon in the image's upper left corner. The effect will be to make the subject stand out against a fuzzy backdrop.

Additionally, a slider can be found under "edit" that allows you to change the blur's intensity. However, you may change the focus to another area of the picture by touching on the yellow autofocus box.

Press "done" to save your changes when you're happy with them. The good news is that if you make a mistake, you can easily reverse it and go back to the original image.

6. A Walkthrough Of The iPhone 15 Pro Max's 5x Optical Zoom

You can get better shots of distant things and individuals with the iPhone 15 Pro Max compared to its siblings. Using a system of numerous mirrors to extend the focus length, a new telephoto camera achieves an optical zoom of up to 5x, surpassing the 3x magnification seen on the iPhone 15 Pro.

To activate the new function, just press the 5x button located at the viewfinder's base when the camera is in picture mode. You may squeeze the screen to activate digital zoom up to 25x, but keep in mind that picture quality decreases as you zoom in more.

7. How To Use The Action Button On The iPhone

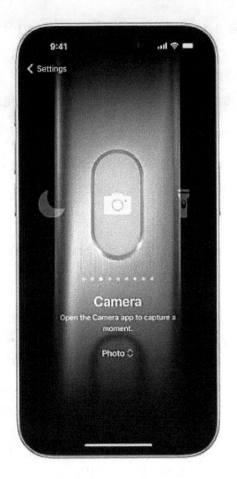

A new button, replacing the ring/silent switch, has been introduced to the iPhone 15 Pro models by Apple. You can change the new button's behavior so it does whatever you want it to instead of just that one thing. As a shortcut, you may program it to launch your preferred app, camera, or flashlight. It also has the ability to be assigned shortcuts if you utilize them.

The internet is rife with ingenious and fascinating ways to press the button, as usual. Some examples include opening and closing curtains, Facetiming a spouse, and locking and unlocking a Tesla. Plus, you always have the option to do nothing or put your phone on quiet if none of that piques your interest.

Adjust the parameters by clicking the action button. Take a look at all the options for what to do next. Additional choices may be accessed using the arrows that are located under each symbol. By pressing the blue button that is beneath the action, you have the ability to create custom shortcuts and accessibility settings.

8. How To Use An External Hard Drive To Capture Video From An iPhone

Mastering ProRes video is a must if you want to follow in Christopher Nolan's footsteps. Though everyone with an iPhone can capture a video, only true experts utilize ProRes, as the name suggests. It is mostly used by film editors in post-production when using programs like Final Cut.

Capturing video with far greater information in terms of tone, color, and motion is basically what this function is all about. Even better, you can record to an external hard drive in 4K at up to 60fps with the iPhone 15 Pro and Pro Max. Since the clips are somewhat huge, there is no way to save them to your phone without severely restricting your storage capacity.

Opening the Camera app, connecting the hard drive to the USB-C connection on your iPhone 15 Pro or 15 Pro Max, turning on ProRes recording, and tapping the record button are all that's needed to begin recording ProRes footage to an external disk. You are now prepared to wow everyone with your unique creation or a video of your mother's celebration. Heck, even Spielberg used personal footage as a starting point.

9. How To Use A Hardwired Internet Connection

The USB-C connector on the iPhone 15 series can do more than just charge your phone; we've previously covered that.

Its capacity to provide a speed boost for streaming games or Netflix is one of those helpful extras. Connect your iPhone 15 to the internet directly using a USB-C to Ethernet converter if your house wifi or 5G isn't enough. An notice confirming that the iPhone has detected the attached device will appear after you do this. Then, in the newly added "Ethernet" area of your settings, you will be able to see details on your connection. Your router details and IP address are shown here.

On a full-fiber broadband network, we were able to get a maximum download speed of 320Mbps after giving it a go. Compared to a MacBook's 800Mbps cable download speed, it was a substantial improvement, but it was still far slower than wifi.

This capability existed already on earlier iPhones with Lightning connectors, but if you already own the USB-C adapter—say, for your laptop—you could already have it on hand.